Watch Me Grow © copyright 2022 by Josalyn Thomas. All rights reserved. No parts of this book may be reproduced in any form whatsoever, by photography or xerography or by any other means, by broadcast or transmission, by translation into any language, nor by recording electronically or otherwise, without permission in writing from the author, except by a reviewer, who may quote brief passages in critical articles or reviews.

Illustration by Lindsey Bailey
Production editor: Crown Shepherd

ISBN 13: 978-0-578-31805-9
Library of Congress Catalog Number: 2021922993
Printed in the United States of America
First Printing: 2022
22 23 24 25 26   5 4 3 2 1

CrownTheWriter
www.crownthewriter.com

To Order, visit www.expandingmindscc.com. Reseller discounts available.

Contact Josalyn Thomas at www.expandingmindscc.com for school visits, speaking engagements, freelance writing projects, and interviews.

This book is dedicated to my children Ahmad & Kimora and to all the children I've had the pleasure of teaching and watching grow over the years.

Watch me grow from a seed
in the soil planted deep.

There I find warmth and sink into the dark earth.

Watch me breathe in the earth,

spreading myself long and wide.

and deepen my understanding of life.

drenching me in life,
giving me all the power.

Watch me blossom and spread wide when the sun hits me right,

revealing my true colors and
releasing my true light.

something that can change the world.

Watch me fill hungry tummies,

helping kids grow big and strong.

Watch me return to the earth to be reborn,

starting my life-giving cycle again.

ABOUT THE AUTHOR

Josalyn Thomas was born and raised on the Southside of Minneapolis, Minnesota. She grew her love for gardening and giving back to her community with her local community center "Waite House." Josalyn is a mother to Ahmad and Kimora; she has also had the pleasure of being her children's first teacher. Being her children's first teacher inspired Josalyn to make a change in her community by becoming a teacher. She thanks all the children and families that have trusted her with their children along this journey.

ABOUT THE ILLUSTRATOR

Lindsey Bailey is an artist and illustrator based in Mississippi. She graduated from Mississippi State University in 2009 with a BFA in Graphic Design. She has worked on editorial illustration, character design, book covers, children's books, and portraits for clients including Black Dog & Leventhal Publishers, Bleacher Report, Rebel Girls, The Georgia Review and ESPN. Her work centers on the representation of people of color, specifically Black women and children.